Shield of Love
Prayers of Protection for Kids

Published in 2023
First published in the UK by THP Kidz Zone
An imprint of Tamarind Hill Press Limited
Newton Aycliffe, County Durham, DL5 6XP
Copyrights © THP Kidz Zone
All rights reserved

Written by Tara Robertson

ISBN Paperback: 978-1-915161-23-9

Printed and manufactured by Lightning Source LLC

Shield of Love

Tara Robertson

Dear God,
Thank you for your constant protection and care. Please continue to watch over me and keep me safe always.
Amen.

Dear God,
Please protect my family and keep us safe, peaceful, and happy.
Amen.

Dear God,
Please protect my school and keep me and my classmates safe and happy.
Amen.

Dear God,

Please protect my pets and keep them safe and healthy.

Amen.

Dear God,

Please protect my home and keep it safe and cosy.

Amen.

Dear God,
Please protect me when I'm traveling and keep me safe on car rides and trips.
Amen.

Dear God,
Please protect me from sickness and help me heal if I get ill.
Amen.

Dear God,
Please protect my grandmother and keep her safe and strong.
Amen.

Dear God,

Please protect me from fear and help me to have faith in your love and protection.

.Amen.

Dear God,
Please protect me from accidents and keep me safe when I'm playing and exploring.
Amen.

Dear God,

Please protect me from bad dreams and help me to sleep peacefully at night. Amen.

www.ingramcontent.com/pod-product-compliance
Lightning Source LLC
Chambersburg PA
CBHW041644220426
43661CB00018B/1296